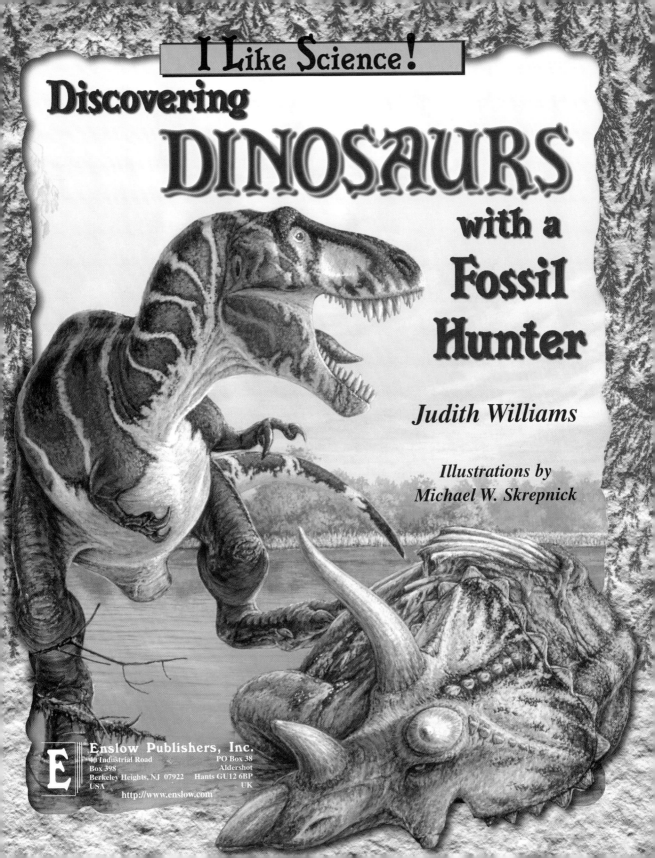

# I Like Science!

# Discovering DINOSAURS with a Fossil Hunter

*Judith Williams*

*Illustrations by*
*Michael W. Skrepnick*

**Enslow Publishers, Inc.**
40 Industrial Road          PO Box 38
Box 398                     Aldershot
Berkeley Heights, NJ 07922  Hants GU12 6BP
USA                         UK
http://www.enslow.com

# Contents

How do we find out facts about
dinosaurs? . . . . . . . . . . . . . . . . . 3

Meet paleontologist Phil Currie . . . . . 4

How are fossils found? . . . . . . . . . . . . 6

What do paleontologists
do next? . . . . . . . . . . . . . . . . . 8

What do fossils show us? . . . . . . . . . . 10

Did dinosaurs come from eggs? . . . . . 12

Did all baby dinosaurs stay in
the nest? . . . . . . . . . . . . . . . . . . 14

Did all dinosaurs eat meat? . . . . . . . . 16

Did meat-eating dinosaurs live in
groups? . . . . . . . . . . . . . . . . . . . 18

How are plant fossils formed? . . . . . . 21

Learn More: Books and Web Sites . . . 23

Index . . . . . . . . . . . . . . . . . . . . . . 24

# Words to Know

**fossil  (FOSS ul)—What is left from a plant or animal that lived long ago.**

**pack  (PAK)—A group of animals that lives and hunts together, like wolves.**

**paleontologist  (pail ee on TOL oh gist)—A scientist who studies fossils and life from long ago.**

**plaster  (PLAS tur)—A powder mixed with water that gets hard when it dries.**

**skeleton  (SKEL a ton)—All the bones that make up an animal's body.**

**tyrannosaur  (tie RAN oh sor)—A kind of meat-eating dinosaur, such as *T. rex*.**

# How do we find out facts about dinosaurs?

Scientists start by asking questions.

How is one dinosaur different from another? What things are the same? That is how scientists learn!

duck-billed dinosaurs

# Meet paleontologist Phil Currie.

He is a dinosaur scientist. He has liked dinosaurs since he was young. Now, learning about them is his job.

What does he do?

4

dinosaur footprint

He finds fossils and measures bones. He sorts the facts. He wants to know how dinosaurs lived.

5

# How do paleontologists find dinosaur fossils?

Paleontologists look for bones lying on the ground. Often, only part of the fossil shows.

Gobi Desert in Asia

If they dig, they might get lucky and find the rest of the skeleton.

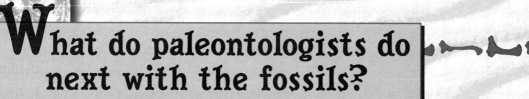

# What do paleontologists do next with the fossils?

They cover the fossils in wet plaster. When the plaster dries, it turns hard.

dinosaur bones inside

Then the fossil is safe to be moved.

Next it is cleaned and studied
in the lab.

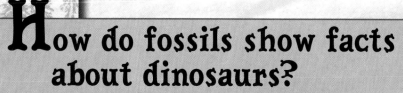

Fossils tell stories about dinosaur lives. Each bone and tooth shows many things.

Diplodocus (dih PLAHD oh kus) family

To paleontologists, bones answer questions. If you were a paleontologist, what questions would *you* ask?

# Did dinosaurs come from eggs?

Yes, just like birds,
dinosaurs laid eggs.

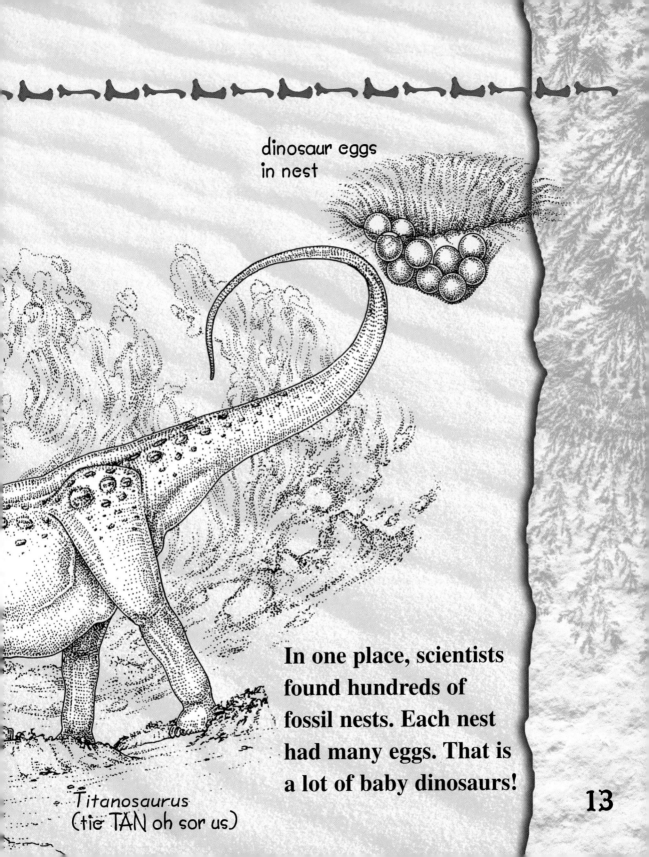

dinosaur eggs
in nest

In one place, scientists
found hundreds of
fossil nests. Each nest
had many eggs. That is
a lot of baby dinosaurs!

Titanosaurus
(tie TAN oh sor us)

# Did all baby dinosaurs stay in the nest when they were young?

Tyrannosaurus babies may have had feathers.

Maybe they did not. Meat-eating dinosaurs may have left the nest after they hatched. They could run. They could hunt. They were busy right away!

# Did all dinosaurs eat meat?

Iguanodon (ih GWAHN oh don)

No, most dinosaurs ate only plants. Scientists look at plant fossils. The fossils show what these dinosaurs ate.

Some dinosaurs ate meat—usually other dinosaurs. But they would eat any animal they could catch.

Gorgosaurus
(GOR goh SOR us)

Centrosaurus
(SEN troh SOR us)

Paleontologist Phil found many tyrannosaur fossils in one place. Some were young. Some were adults.

18

He thinks these dinosaurs lived in groups, called packs. Maybe young dinosaurs helped the adults hunt.

Hypacrosaurus
(hie PAK roh SOR us)

Albertosaurus
(al BURT oh SOR us) pack

Paleontologists like Phil Currie are busy thinking of many more questions about dinosaurs. They are looking for answers, too.

Good-bye, paleontologist Phil, and good luck!

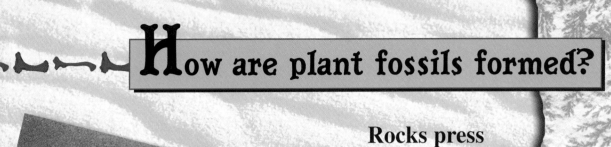

Rocks press down on plants, just as they did on dinosaur bones. You can see how this works.

1. Take two sheets of plain white paper. Put a leaf between the sheets of paper.

21

**2. With a colored pencil, color the top sheet over the leaf.**

**3. The shape looks like a plant fossil.**

**Well done!**

## Books

Davis, Lee. *Dinosaur Dinners*. New York: DK Publishing Inc., 1998.

Dingus, Lowell, and Mark A. Norell. *Searching for Velociraptor*. New York: HarperCollins Children's Book Group, 1996.

Dodson, Peter. *An Alphabet of Dinosaurs*. New York: Scholastic Inc., 1995.

Tanaka, Shelley. *Graveyards of the Dinosaurs*. Toronto: Scholastic/Madison Press Books, 1998.

Thomson, Ruth. *Dinosaur's Day*. London: DK Publishing, Inc., 2000.

Zoehfeld, Kathleen Weidner. *Dinosaur Babies*. New York: HarperCollins Publishers, 1999.

## Web Sites

**National Geographic Kids**
<http://www.nationalgeographic.com/ngkids/0005/dino/>

**The Children's Museum of Indianapolis**
<http://childrensmuseum.org/kinetosaur/index.html>

**Discovery Kids**
<http://kids.discovery.com/fansites/prehistoric/
prehistoric.html>

# Index

baby dinosaurs, 13, 14
bones, 5, 6, 10, 11

Currie, Phil, 4, 18–19, 20

eggs, 12, 13

feathers, 14
fossil, 5, 6, 8, 10, 13, 16, 18, 20, 21, 22

lab, 9

meat eaters, 15, 16

nest, 13, 14, 15

pack, 19
paleontologist, 4, 6, 8, 11, 18, 20
plants, 16, 21, 22
plaster, 8

skeleton, 7

tyrannosaur, 18

❧ *For Michael* ❧

**Series Literacy Consultant:**
Allan A. De Fina, Ph.D.
Past President of the New Jersey Reading Association
Professor, Department of Literacy Education
New Jersey City University

**Science Consultant:**
Philip J. Currie, Ph.D., Curator of Dinosaur Research
Royal Tyrrell Museum, Alberta, Canada
*Dr. Currie says, "I wish there had been a book like this when I was young!"*

**Note to Teachers and Parents:** The *I Like Science!* series supports the National Science Education Standards for K-4 science, including content standards "Science as a human endeavor" and "Science as inquiry." The Words to Know section introduces subject-specific vocabulary, including pronunciation and definitions. Early readers may require help with these new words.

**Library of Congress Cataloging-in-Publication Data**

Williams, Judith (Judith A.)
    Discovering dinosaurs with a fossil hunter / Judith Williams.
        p. cm. — (I like science!)
    Summary: Briefly explains the work of paleontologists, scientists who learn about dinosaurs by studying fossils.
    Includes bibliographical references and index.
    ISBN 0-7660-2267-6
    1. Paleontology—Juvenile literature. 2. Fossils—Juvenile literature. [1. Paleontology. 2. Fossils.] I. Title. II. Series.
QE714.5.W55 2004
567.9—dc21
                    2003003613

Printed in the United States of America

10 9 8 7 6 5 4 3 2 1

**To Our Readers:** We have done our best to make sure all Internet Addresses in this book were active and appropriate when we went to press. However, the author and the publisher have no control over and assume no liability for the material available on those Internet sites or on other Web sites they may link to. Any comments or suggestions can be sent by e-mail to comments@ enslow.com or to the address on the back cover.

**Illustration Credits:** © Michael W. Skrepnick

**All Photos** © Michael W. Skrepnick 1990–2003, except Neg. no. 18552, Courtesy the Library, American Museum of Natural History, p. 2; Judith Williams, p. 4.

**Cover Illustration:** Michael W. Skrepnick
*Tyrannosaurus* and *Triceratops*